EDUCATION AS SERVICE

First published 1912
This edition published by Lector House in 2024

ISBN: 978-93-6138-744-9

Lector House LLP
Registered Office: H. No. 96, Block C, Tomar Colony,
Burari, Delhi – 110084, India
info@lectorhouse.com
www.lectorhouse.com

EDUCATION AS SERVICE

JIDDU KRISHNAMURTI

2024

LECTOR HOUSE

LECTOR HOUSE LLP

EDUCATION AS SERVICE

BY

J. KRISHNAMURTI

(ALCYONE)

Introduction.

In long past lives the author of this little book had much to do with educational work, and he seems to have brought over with him an intense interest in education. During his short visits to Benares, he paid an alert attention to many of the details of the work carried on in the Central Hindu College, observing and asking questions, noting the good feeling between teachers and students, so different from his own school experiences in Southern India. He appears to have been brooding over the question, and has, in this booklet, held up the educational ideals which appear to him to be necessary for the improvement of the present system.

The position of the teacher must be raised to that which it used to occupy in India, so that to sit in the teacher's chair will be a badge of social honour. His work must be seen as belonging to the great Teaching Department in the Government of our world, and his relation with his pupils must be a copy of the relation between a Master and His disciples. Love, protective and elevating on the one side, must be met with love, confiding and trustful on the other. This is, in truth, the old Hindu ideal, exaggerated as it may seem to be to-day and if it be possible, in any country to rebuild this ideal, it should be by an Indian for Indians. Hence there is, at the back of the author's mind, a dream of a future College and School, wherein this ideal may be materialised—a Theosophical College and School, because the ancient Indian ideals now draw their life from Theosophy which alone can shape the new vessels for the ancient elixir of life.

Punishment must disappear—not only the old brutality of the cane, but all the forms of coercion that make hypocrites instead of honourable and manly youths. The teacher must embody the ideal, and the boy be drawn, by admiration and love, to copy it. Those who know how swiftly the unspoiled child responds to a noble ideal will realise how potent may be the influence of a teacher, who stimulates by a high example and rules by the sceptre of love instead of by the rod of fear. Besides, the One Life is in teacher and taught, as Alcyone reminds us, and to that Life, which is Divine, all things are possible.

Education must be shaped to meet the individual needs of the child, and not by a Government Procrustes' bed, to fit which some are dragged well-nigh asunder and others are chopped down. The capacities of the child, the line they fit him to pursue, these must guide his education. In all, the child's interest must be paramount; the true teacher exists to serve.

The school must be a centre of good and joyous influences, radiating from it to the neighbourhood. Studies and games must all be turned to the building of character, to the making of the good citizen, the lover of his country.

Thus dreams the boy, who is to become a teacher, of the possibilities the future may unfold. May he realise, in the strength of a noble Manhood, the pure visions of his youth, and embody a Power which shall make earth's deserts rejoice and blossom as the rose.

ANNIE BESANT.

To the
Supreme Teacher
and to
Those who follow him

Foreword.

Many of the suggestions made in this little book come from my own memories of early school life; and my own experience since of the methods used in Occult training has shown me how much happier boys' lives might be made than they usually are. I have myself experienced both the right way of teaching and the wrong way, and therefore I want to help others towards the right way. I write upon the subject because it is one which is very near to the heart of my Master, and much of what I say is but an imperfect echo of what I have heard from Him. Then again, during the last two years, I have seen much of the work done in the Central Hindu College at Benares by Mr. G.S. Arundale and his devoted band of helpers. I have seen teachers glad to spend their time and energies in continual service of those whom they regard as their younger brothers. I have also watched the boys, in their turn, showing a reverence and an affectionate gratitude to their teachers that I had never thought possible.

Though many people may think the ideals put forward are entirely beyond the average teacher, and cannot be put into practice in ordinary schools, I can thus point at least to one institution in which I have seen many of the suggestions made in this book actually carried out. It may be that some of them *are*, at present, beyond most schools; but they will be recognised and practised as soon as teachers realise them as desirable, and have a proper understanding of the importance of their office.

Most of the recommendations apply, I think, to all countries, and to all religions, and are intended to sound the note of our common brotherhood, irrespective of religion or caste, race or colour. If the unity of life and the oneness of its purpose could be clearly taught to the young in schools, how much brighter would be our hopes for the future! The mutual distrust of races and nations would disappear, if the children were trained in mutual love and sympathy as members of one great family of children all over the world, instead of being taught to glory only in their own traditions and to despise those of others. True patriotism is a beautiful quality in children, for it means unselfishness of purpose and enthusiasm for great ideals; but that is false patriotism which shows itself in contempt for other nations. There are, I am told, many organisations within the various nations of the world, intended to inspire the children with a love for their country and a desire to serve her, and that is surely good; but I wonder when there will be an international organisation to give the children of all nations common ideals also, and a knowledge of the real foundation of right action, the Brotherhood of Man.

I desire to thank my dear mother, Mrs. Annie Besant, for the help she has given me while I have been writing this little book, and also my dear friend, Mr. G.S. Arundale—with whom I have often talked on the subject—for many useful suggestions.

J. Krishnamurti.

Contents

The Teacher.

In *At the Feet of the Master* I have written down the instructions given to me by my Master in preparing me to learn how best to be useful to those around me. All who have read the book will know how inspiring the Master's words are, and how they make each person who reads them long to train himself for the service of others. I know myself how much I have been helped by the loving care of those to whom I look for guidance, and I am eager to pass on to others the help I have obtained from them.

It seems to me that the Master's instructions can be universally applied. They are useful not only to those who are definitely trying to tread the path which leads to Initiation, but also to all who, while still doing the ordinary work of the world, are anxious to do their duty earnestly and unselfishly. One of the noblest forms of work is that of the teacher; let us see what light is thrown upon it by the words of the Master.

I will take the four Qualifications which have been given in *At the Feet of the Master*, and will try to show how they can be applied to the life of the teacher and of the students, and to the relations which should exist between them.

The most important Qualification in education is Love, and I will take that first.

It is sad that in modern days the office of a teacher has not been regarded as on a level with other learned professions. Any one has been thought good enough to be a teacher, and as a result little honour has been paid to him. Naturally, therefore, the cleverest boys are not drawn towards that profession. But really the office of the teacher is the most sacred and the most important to the nation, because it builds the characters of the boys and girls who will be its future citizens. In olden days this office was thought so holy that only priests were teachers and the school was a part of the temple. In India the trust in the teacher was so great that the parents gave over their sons completely to him for many years, and teacher and students lived together as a family. Because this happy relation should be brought back again, I put Love first among the Qualifications which a teacher ought to have. If India is to become again the great nation which we all hope to see, this old happy relation must be re-established.

I.

Love.

My Master taught me that Love will enable a man to acquire all other qualities and that "all the rest without it would never be sufficient." Therefore no person ought to be a teacher—ought to be allowed to be a teacher—unless he has shown in his daily life that Love is the strongest quality of his nature. It may be asked: How are we to find out whether a person possesses Love to a sufficient degree to make him worthy to be a teacher? Just as a boy shows his natural capacities at an early age for one profession or another, so a particularly strong love-nature would mark a boy out as specially fitted to be an instructor. Such boys should be definitely trained for the office of the teacher just as boys are trained for other professions.

Boys who are preparing for all careers live a common life in the same school, and they can only become useful to the nation as men, if their school life is happy. A young child is naturally happy, and if that happiness is allowed to go on and grow in the school, and at home, then he will become a man who will make others happy. A teacher full of love and sympathy will attract the boys and make their school life a pleasant one. My Master once said that "children are very eager to learn and if a teacher cannot interest them and make them love their lessons, he is not fit to be a teacher and should choose another profession." He has said also: "Those who are mine love to teach and to serve. They long for an opportunity of service as a hungry man longs for food, and they are always watching for it. Their hearts are so full of the divine Love that it must be always overflowing in love for those around them. Only such are fit to be teachers—those to whom teaching is not only a holy and imperative duty, but also the greatest of pleasures."

A sympathetic teacher draws out all the good qualities in his pupils, and his gentleness prevents them from being afraid of him. Each boy then shows himself just as he is, and the teacher is able to see the line best suited to him and to help him to follow it. To such a teacher a boy will come with all his difficulties, knowing that he will be met with sympathy and kindness, and, instead of hiding his weaknesses, he will be glad to tell everything to one of whose loving help he is sure. The good teacher remembers his own youth, and so can feel with the boy who comes to him. My Master said: "He who has forgotten his childhood and lost sympathy with the children is not a man who can teach them or help them."

This love of the teacher for his pupil, protecting and helping him, will bring out love from the pupil in turn, and as he looks up to his teacher this love will take the form of reverence. Reverence, beginning in this way with the boy, will grow as he grows older, and will become the habit of seeing and reverencing greatness, and so perhaps in time may lead him to the Feet of the Master. The love of the boy to the teacher will make him docile and easy to guide, and so the question of punishment will never arise. Thus one great cause of fear which at present poisons all the relations between the teacher and his pupil will vanish. Those of us who have the happiness of being pupils of the true Masters know what this relation ought to be. We know the wonderful patience, gentleness and sympathy with which They always meet us, even when we may have made mistakes or have been weak.

Yet there is much more difference between Them and us than between the ordinary teacher and his pupil. When the teacher has learned to look upon his office as dedicating him to the service of the nation, as the Master has dedicated Himself to the service of humanity, then he will become part of the great Teaching Department of the world, to which belongs my own beloved Master—the Department of which the supreme Teacher of Gods and men is the august Head.

It may be said that many boys could not be managed in this way. The answer is that such boys have been already spoiled by bad treatment. Even so, they must be slowly improved by greater patience and constant love. This plan has already proved successful when tried.

Living in this atmosphere of love during school hours, the boy will become a better son and a better brother at home, and will bring home with him a feeling of life and vigour, instead of coming home, as he generally does now, depressed and tired. When he, in turn, becomes the head of a household, he will fill it with the love in which he has been brought up, and so the happiness will go on spreading and increasing, generation after generation. Such a boy when he becomes a father, will not look on his son, as so many do now, from a purely selfish point of view, as though he were merely a piece of property—as though the son existed for the sake of the father. Some parents seem to regard their children only as a means of increasing the prosperity and reputation of the family by the professions which they may adopt or the marriages that they may make, without considering in the least the wishes of the children themselves. The wise father will consult his boy as a friend, will take pains to find out what his wishes are, and will help him with his greater experience to carry out those wishes wisely, remembering always that his son is an ego who has come to the father to give him the opportunity of making good karma by aiding the son in his progress. He will never forget that though his son's body may be young, the soul within is as old as his own, and must therefore be treated with respect as well as affection.

Love both at home and in the school will naturally show itself in continual small acts of service, and these will form a habit out of which will grow the larger and more heroic acts of service which makes the greatness of a nation.

The Master speaks much on cruelty as a sin against love, and distinguishes between intentional and unintentional cruelty. He says: "Intentional cruelty is purposely to give pain to another living being; and that is the greatest of all sins—the work of a devil rather than a man." The use of the cane must be classed under this, for He says of intentional cruelty: "Many schoolmasters do it habitually." We must also include all words and acts *intended* to wound the feelings of the boy and to hurt his self-respect. In some countries corporal punishment is forbidden, but in most it is still the custom. But my Master said: "These people try to excuse their brutality by saying that it is the custom; but a crime does not cease to be a crime because many commit it. Karma takes no account of custom; and the karma of cruelty is the most terrible of all. In India at least there can be no excuse for such customs, for the duty of harmlessness is well known to all."

The whole idea of what is called "punishment" is not only wrong but foolish. A teacher who tries to frighten his boys into doing what he wishes does not see that they only obey him while he is there, and that as soon as they are out of his sight they will pay no attention to his rules, or even take a pleasure in breaking them because they dislike him. But if he draws them to do what he wants because they love him and wish to please him, they will keep his rules even in his absence, and so make his work much easier. Instead of developing fear and dislike in the characters of the boys, the wise teacher will gain his ends by calling forth from them love and devotion; and so will strengthen all that is good in them, and help them on the road of evolution.

Again, the idea of expulsion, of getting rid of a troublesome boy instead of trying to improve him, is wrong. Even when, for the sake of his companions, a boy has to be separated from them, the good of the boy himself must not be forgotten. In fact, all through, school discipline should be based on the good of the boys and not on the idea of saving trouble to the teacher. The loving teacher does not mind the trouble.

Unintentional cruelty often comes from mere thoughtlessness, and the teacher should be very careful not to be cruel in words or actions from want of thought. Teachers often cause pain by hasty words uttered at a time when they have been disturbed by some outside annoyance, or are trying to attend to some important duty. The teacher may forget the incident or pass it over as trivial, but in many such cases a sensitive boy has been wounded, and he broods over the words and ends by imagining all sorts of foolish exaggerations. In this way many misunderstandings arise between teachers and boys, and though the boys must learn to be patient and generous, and to realise that the teacher is anxious to help all as much as he can, the teacher in his turn must always be on the alert to watch his words, and to allow nothing but gentleness to shine out from his speech and actions, however busy he may be.

If the teacher is always gentle to the boys, who are younger and weaker than himself, it will be easy for him to teach them the important lesson of kindness to little children, animals, birds and other living creatures. The older boys, who themselves are gentle and tactful, should be encouraged to observe the condition of the animals they see in the streets, and if they see any act of cruelty, to beg the doer of it very politely and gently, to treat the animal more kindly. The boys should be taught that nothing which involves the hunting and killing of animals should be called sport. That word ought to be kept for manly games and exercises, and not used for the wounding and killing of animals. My Master says: "The fate of the cruel must fall also upon all who go out intentionally to kill God's creatures and call it sport."

I do not think that teachers realise the harm and the suffering caused by gossip, which the Master calls a sin against love. Teachers should be very careful not to make difficulties for their boys by gossiping about them. No boy should ever be allowed to have a bad name in the school, and it should be the rule that no one may speak ill of any other member of the school whether teacher or boy.

My Master points out that by talking about a person's faults, we not only strengthen those faults in him, but also fill our own minds with evil thoughts. There is only one way of really getting rid of our lower nature, and that is by strengthening the higher. And while it is the duty of the teacher to understand the weaknesses of those placed in his charge he must realise that he will destroy the lower nature only by surrounding the boy with his love, thus stimulating the higher and nobler qualities till there is no place left for the weaknesses. The more the teacher gossips about the faults of the boys, the more harm he does, and, except during a consultation with his fellow teachers as to the best methods of helping individual boys out of their weaknesses, he should never talk about a boy's defects.

The boys must also be taught the cruelty of gossip among themselves. I know many a boy whose life at school has been made miserable because his companions have been thoughtless and unkind, and the teacher either has not noticed his unhappiness, or has not understood how to explain to the boys the nature of the harm they were doing. Boys frequently take hold of some peculiarity in speech or in dress, or of some mistake which has been made, and, not realising the pain they cause, carelessly torture their unfortunate schoolfellow with unkind allusions. In this case the mischief is due chiefly to ignorance, and if the teacher has influence over the boys, and gently explains to them what pain they are giving they will quickly stop.

They must be taught, too, that nothing which causes suffering or annoyance to another can ever be the right thing to do, nor can it ever be amusing to any right-minded boy. Some children seem to find pleasure in teasing or annoying others, but that is only because they are ignorant. When they understand, they will never again be so unbrotherly.

In every class-room these words of my Master should be put up in a prominent place: "Never speak ill of any one; refuse to listen when anyone else speaks ill of another, but gently say: 'Perhaps this is not true, and even if it is, it is kinder not to speak of it.'"

There are crimes against love which are not recognised as crimes, and which are unfortunately very common. A teacher must use discretion in dealing with these, but should teach a doctrine of love so far as he is permitted, and may at least set a good example himself. Three of these are put by my Master under the head of cruelties caused by superstition.

1. Animal sacrifice. Among civilised nations this is now found only in India, and is tending to disappear even there. Parents and teachers should tell their boys that no custom which is cruel is really part of any true religion. For we have seen that religion teaches unity, and therefore kindness and gentleness to everything that feels. God cannot therefore be served by cruelty and the killing of helpless creatures. If Indian boys learn this lesson of love in school they will, when they become men, put an end entirely to this cruel superstition.

2. Much more widely spread is what my Master calls "the still more cruel superstition that man needs flesh for food." This is a matter that concerns the parent more than the teacher, but at least the teacher may gradually lead his boys to see the cruelty involved in killing animals for food. Then, even if the boy is obliged to eat meat at home, he will give it up when he is a man, and will give his own children a better opportunity than he himself had. If parents at home and teachers at school would train young children in the duty of loving and protecting all living creatures, the world would be much happier than it is at present.

3. "The treatment which superstition has meted out to the depressed classes in our beloved India," says the Master, is a proof that "this evil quality can breed heartless cruelty even among those who know the duty of Brotherhood." To get rid of this form of cruelty every boy must be taught the great lesson of love, and much can be done for this in school as well as at home. The boy at school has many special opportunities of learning this lesson, and the teacher should point out the duty of showing courtesy and kindness to all who are in inferior positions, as well as to the poor whom he may meet outside. All who know the truth of reincarnation should realise that they are members of one great family, in which some are younger brethren and some elder. Boys must be taught to show gentleness and consideration to servants, and to all who are below them in social position; caste was not intended to promote pride and rudeness, and Manu teaches that servants

should be treated as the children of the family.

A great part of the teacher's work lies in the playground, and the teacher who does not play with his boys will never quite win their hearts. Indian boys as a rule do not play enough, and time should be given for games during the school day. Even the teachers who have not learned to play in their youth should come to the playground and show interest in the games, thus sharing in this part of the boy's education.

In schools where there are boarding-houses the love of the teacher is especially necessary, for in them the boarding-house must take the place of the home, and a family feeling must be created there. Bright and affectionate teachers will be looked on as elder brothers, and difficulties which escape rules will be got rid of by love.

In fact, all the many activities of school life should be made into channels through which affection can run between teacher and pupil, and the more channels there are the better it will be for both. As the boy grows older these channels will naturally become more numerous, and the love of the school will become the friendship of manhood. Thus love will have her perfect work.

Love on the physical plane has many forms. We have the love of husband and wife, parents and children, brothers and sisters, the affection between relatives and friends. But all these are blended and enriched in the love of the Master to His disciple. The Master gives to His pupil the gentleness and protection of a mother, the strength of a father, the understanding of a brother or a sister, the encouragement of a relative or a friend, and He is one with His pupil and His pupil is a part of Him. Besides this, the Master knows His pupil's past, and His pupil's future, and guides him through the present from the past into the future. The pupil knows but little beyond the present, and he does not understand that great love which draws its inspiration from the memory of the past and shapes itself to mould the powers of the future. He may even sometimes doubt the wisdom of the love which guides itself according to a pattern which his eyes cannot see.

That which I have said above may seem a very high ideal for the relation between a teacher and pupil down here. Yet the difference between them is less than the difference between a Master and His disciple. The lower relation should be a faint reflection of the higher, and at least the teacher may set the higher before himself as an ideal. Such an ideal will lift all his work into a higher world, and all school life will be made happier and better because the teacher has set it before him.

II.

Discrimination.

The next very necessary qualification for the teacher is Discrimination. My Master said that the most important knowledge was "the knowledge of God's plan for men, for God has a plan, and that plan is evolution." Each boy has his own place in evolution, and the teacher must try to see what that place is, and how he can best help the boy in that place. This is what the Hindus call Dharma, and it is the teacher's duty to find out the boy's dharma and to help him to fulfil it. In other words, the teaching given to the boy should be that which is suitable for him, and the teacher must use discrimination in choosing the teaching, and in his way of giving it. Under these conditions, the boy's progress would be following out the tendencies made in past lives, and would really be remembering the things he knew before. "The method of evolution," as a great Master said, "is a constant dipping down into matter under the law of readjustment," *i.e.* by reincarnation and karma. Unless the teacher knows these truths, he cannot work with evolution as he should do, and much of his time and of his pupil's time will be wasted. It is this ignorance which causes such small results to be seen, after many years at school, and which leaves the boy himself so ignorant of the great truths which he needs to guide his conduct in life.

Discrimination is wanted in the choice of subjects and in the way in which they are taught. First in importance come religion and morals, and these must not only be taught as subjects but must be made both the foundation and the atmosphere of school life, for these are equally wanted by every boy, no matter what he is to do later in life. Religion teaches us that we are all part of One Self, and that we ought therefore help one another. My Master said that people "try to invent ways for themselves which they think will be pleasant for themselves, not understanding that all are one, and that therefore only what the One wills can ever be really pleasant for anyone." And He also said: "You can help your brother through that which you have in common with him, and that is the Divine life." To teach this is to teach religion, and to live it is to lead the religious life.

At present the value of the set moral teaching is largely made useless by the arrangements of the school. The school day should always open with something of the nature of a religious service, striking the note of a common purpose and a common life, so that the boys, who are all coming from different homes and different ways of living may be tuned to unity in the school. It is a good plan to begin with a little music or singing so that the boys, who often come rushing in from hastily taken food, may quiet down and begin the school day in an orderly way. After this should come a prayer and a very short but beautiful address, placing an ideal before the boys.

But if these ideals are to be useful, they must be practised all through the school day, so that the spirit of the religious period may run through the lessons and the games. For example, the duty of the strong to help the weak is taught in the religious hour, and yet for the rest of the day the strong are set to outstrip the weak, and are given valuable prizes for their success in doing so. These prizes make many boys jealous and discourage others, they stimulate the spirit of struggle. The Central Hindu College Brotherhood has for its motto: "The ideal reward is an increased power to love and to serve." If the prizes for good work and conduct and for helping others were positions of greater trust and power of helping, this motto would be carried out. In fact, in school honour should be given to character and helpfulness rather than to strength of mind and body; strength ought to be trained and developed, but not rewarded for merely outstripping the weak. Such a school life will send out into the world men who will think more of filling places of usefulness to the nation than of merely gaining money and power for themselves.

An important part of moral teaching lies in the training of the boy in patriotism—love of country. The above plan of teaching the boy to be of service in the little family of the school, will naturally widen out into service in the large family of the nation. This will also influence the boy in his choice of a profession, for he will think of the nation as his family, and will try to fill a useful place in the national life. But great care must be taken in teaching patriotism not to let the boys slip into hatred of other nations, as so often happens. This is especially important in India, where both Indian and

English teachers should try to make good feeling between the two races living side by side, so that they may join in common work for the one Empire.

Discrimination may also be shown in the arrangement of lessons, the most difficult subjects being taken early in the day, as far as possible. For even with the best and most carefully arranged teaching a boy will be more tired at the end of the school day than at the beginning.

Discrimination is also wanted in the method of teaching, and in the amount of time given to mental and physical education. The care of the body and its development are of the first importance, for without a healthy body all teaching is wasted. It should be remembered that the boy can go on, learning all his life, if he is wise enough to wish to do so; but it is only during the years of growth that he can build up a healthy physical body in which to spend that life. Therefore during those early years the healthy development of that physical body must be absolutely the first consideration, and anything that cannot be learned compatibly with that must for the time remain unlearned. The strain on the boy's mind—and particularly on those of very young boys—is far too great and lasts far too long; the lesson period should be broken up, and the teacher should be very careful to watch the boys and to see that they do not become tired. His wish to prevent this strain will make him think out new ways of teaching, which will make the lessons very interesting; for a boy who is interested does not easily become tired. I myself remember how tired we used to be when we reached home, far too tired to do anything but lie about. But the Indian boy is not allowed to rest even when he comes home, for he has then to begin home lessons, often with a tutor, when he ought to be at rest or play. These home lessons begin again in the morning, before he goes to school, and the result is that he looks on his lessons as a hardship instead of a pleasure. Much of this homework is done by a very bad light and the boy's eyes suffer much. All home lessons should be abolished; home work burns the candle at both ends, and makes the boy's life a slavery. School hours are quite long enough, and an intelligent teacher can impart in them quite as much as any boy ought to learn in one day. What cannot be taught within those hours should be postponed until the next day.

We see the result of all this overstrain in the prevalence of eye-diseases in India. Western countries set us a good example in the physical training of their boys, who leave school strong and healthy. I have heard in England that in the poorer schools the children are often inspected by a doctor so that any eye-disease or other defect is found out at once before it becomes serious. I wonder how many boys in India are called stupid merely because they are suffering from some eye or ear trouble.

Discrimination should also be shown in deciding the length of the waking and sleeping times. These vary, of course, with age and to some extent perhaps with temperament. No boy should have less than nine or ten hours of sleep; when growth ceases, eight hours would generally be enough. A boy grows most during his sleep, so that the time is not in the least wasted.

Few people realise how much a boy is affected by his surroundings, by the things on which his eyes are continually resting. The emotions and the mind are largely trained through the eye, and bare walls, or, still worse, ugly pictures are distinctly harmful. It is true that beautiful surroundings sometimes cost a little more than ugly ones, but the money is well spent. In some things only trouble is needed in choosing, for an ugly picture costs as much as a pretty one. Perfect cleanliness is also absolutely necessary, and teachers should be constantly on the watch to see that it is maintained. The Master said about the body: "Keep it strictly clean always; even from the minutest speck of dirt." Both teachers and students should be very clean and neat in their dress, thus helping to preserve the general beauty of the school surroundings. In all these things careful discrimination is wanted.

If a boy is weak in a particular subject, or is not attracted by some subject which he is obliged to learn, a discriminating teacher will sometimes help him by suggesting to him to teach it to one who knows less than he does. The wish to help the younger boy will make the elder eager to learn more, and that which was a toil becomes a pleasure. A clever teacher will think of many such ways of helping his boys.

If discrimination has been shown, as suggested in a preceding paragraph, in choosing the best and most helpful boys for positions of trust, it will be easy to teach the younger boys to look up to and wish to please them. The wish to please a loved and admired elder is one of the strongest motives in a boy, and this should be used to encourage good conduct, instead of using punishment to drive boys away from what is bad. If the teacher can succeed in attracting this love and admiration to himself, he will remain a helper to his students long after they have become men. I have been told that the boys who were under Dr. Arnold at Rugby continued in after life to turn to him for advice in their troubles and perplexities.

We may perhaps add that discrimination is a most important qualification for those whose duty it is to choose the teachers. High character and the love-nature of which we have already spoken are absolutely necessary if the above suggestions are to be carried out.

III.

Desirelessness.

The next qualification to be considered is Desirelessness.

There are many difficulties in the way of the teacher when he tries to acquire desirelessness, and it also requires special consideration from the standpoint of the student.

As has been said in *At the Feet of the Master*: "In the light of His holy Presence all desire dies, *but* the desire to be like Him." It is also said in the Bhagavad Gita that all desire dies "when once the Supreme is seen." This is the ideal at which to aim, that the One Will shall take the place of changing desires. This Will is seen in our dharma, and in a true teacher, one whose dharma is teaching, his one desire will be to teach, and to teach well. In fact, unless this desire is felt, teaching is not his dharma, for the presence of this desire is inseparable from real capacity to teach.

We have already said that little honour, unfortunately, is attached to the post of a teacher, and that a man often takes the position because he can get nothing else, instead of because he really wants to teach, and knows that he can teach. The result is that he thinks more about salary than anything else, and is always looking about for the chance of a higher salary. This becomes his chief desire. While the teacher is no doubt partly to blame for this, it is the system which is mostly in fault, for the teacher needs enough to support himself and his family, and this is a right and natural wish on his part. It is the duty of the nation to see that he is not placed in a position in which he is obliged to be always desiring increase of salary, or must take private tuition in order to earn enough to live. Only when this has been done will the teacher feel contented and happy in the position he occupies, and feel the dignity of his office as a teacher, whatever may be his position among other teachers—which is, I fear, now marked chiefly by the amount of his salary. Only the man who is really contented and happy can have his mind free to teach well.

The teacher should not desire to gain credit for himself by forcing a boy along his own line, but should consider the special talent of each boy, and the way in which *he* can gain most success. Too often the teacher, thinking only of his own subject, forgets that the boy has to learn many subjects. The one on which most stress should be laid is the one most suited to the boy's capacity. Unless the teachers co-operate with each other, the boy is too much pressed, for each teacher urges him on in his own subject, and gives him home-lessons in this. There are many teachers, but there is only one boy.

Again, the boy's welfare must be put by the teacher before his own desire to obtain good results in an examination. Sometimes it is better for a boy to remain for another year in a class and master a subject thoroughly rather than to go up for an examination which is really too difficult for him. In such a case it is right to keep him back. But it is not right to keep him back merely for the sake of good results for the teacher. On the other hand, a teacher has sometimes to resist the parents who try to force the boy beyond his strength, and think more of his rising into a higher class than of his really knowing his subjects.

Unless the teacher has desirelessness, his own desires may blind him to the aspirations and capacities of the boys in his care, and he will be frequently imposing his own wishes on them instead of helping them in their natural development. However much a teacher may be attracted towards any profession or any particular set of ideas, he must so develop desirelessness that while he creates in his pupils an enthusiasm for principles, he shall not cramp them within the limits of any particular application of the principles, or allow their generous impulses—unbalanced by experience—to grow into narrow fanaticism. Thus, he should teach the principles of citizenship, but not party politics. He should teach the value of all professions to a nation, if honourably filled, and not the superiority of one profession over another.

IV.

Good Conduct.

There are six points which are summed up by the Master as Good Conduct. These are:

1. Self-control as to the mind
2. Self-control in action
3. Tolerance
4. Cheerfulness
5. One-pointedness
6. Confidence

We will take each of these in turn.

1. *Self-control as to the mind* is a most important qualification for a teacher, for it is principally through the mind that he guides and influences his boys. In the first place it means, as my Master has said, "control of temper, so that you may feel no anger or impatience." It is obvious that much harm will be done to boys if their teacher is often angry and impatient. It is true that this anger and impatience are often caused by the outer conditions of the teacher's life, but this does not prevent their bad effect on the boys. Such feelings, due generally to very small causes, re-act upon the minds of the students, and if the teacher is generally impatient and very often angry, he is building into the character of the boys germs of impatience and anger which may in after life destroy their own happiness, and embitter the lives of their relations and friends.

We have to remember also that the boys themselves often come to school discontented and worried on account of troubles at home, and so both teachers and boys bring with them angry and impatient thoughts, which spread through the school, and make the lessons difficult and unpleasant when they should be easy and full of delight. The short religious service referred to in an early part of this little book should be attended by teachers as well as students, and should act as a kind of door to shut out such undesirable feelings. Then both teachers and students would devote their whole energies to the creation of a happy school, to which all should look forward in the morning, and which all should be sorry to leave at the end of the school day.

The lack of control of temper, it must be remembered, often leads to injustice on the part of the teacher, and therefore to sullenness and want of confidence on the boy, and no boy can make real progress, or be in any real sense happy, unless he has complete confidence in the justice of his elders. Much of the strain of modern school life is due to this lack of confidence, and much time has to be wasted in breaking down barriers which would never have been set up if the teacher had been patient.

Anger and impatience grow out of irritability. It is as necessary for the boy to understand his teacher as for the teacher to understand the boy, and hasty temper is an almost insuperable obstacle in the way of such understanding. "The teacher is angry to-day," "The teacher is irritable to-day," "The teacher is short-tempered to-day," are phrases too often on the lips of boys, and they produce a feeling of discomfort in the class-room that makes harmony and ease impossible. Boys learn to watch their teachers, and to guard themselves against their moods, and so distrust replaces confidence. The value of the teacher depends upon his power of inspiring confidence, and he loses this when he gives way to irritability. This is particularly important with young children, for they are eager to learn and eager to love, and only those who have no business to be teachers would dare to meet such eagerness by anger. It is of course true that younger boys are in many ways more difficult to teach than elder ones; for they have not yet learned how to make efforts, nor how to control and guide them when made. The teacher has therefore to help them much more than the elder boys who have learned largely to help themselves. The chief difficulty is to make the best use of the young energies by finding them continual and interesting employment; if the young enthusiasms are checked harshly instead of being guided sympathetically they will soon die out, and the boy will become dull and discontented.

I have read that youth is full of enthusiasm and ideals, and that these gradually disappear with age, until a man is left with few or none. But it seems to me that enthusiasm, if real, should not die out, and leave cynicism behind, but rather should become stronger and more purposeful with age. The young children coming straight out of the heaven-world have brought with them a feeling of unity, and this feeling should be strengthened in them, so that it may last on through life. Anger and irritability belong only to the separated self, and they drive away the feeling of unity.

Self-control also involves calmness, courage and steadiness. Whatever difficulties the teacher may have either at home or at school, he must learn to face them bravely and cheerfully, not only that he may avoid worry for himself, but also that he may set a good example to his boys, and so help them to become strong and brave. Difficulties are much increased by worrying over them, and by imagining them before they happen—doing what Mrs. Besant once called, "crossing bridges before we come to them." Unless the teacher is cheerful and courageous with his own difficulties, he will not be able to help the boys to meet *their* difficulties bravely. Most obstacles grow small before a contented mind, and boys who bring this to their work will find their studies much easier than if they came to them discontented and worried. Courage and steadiness lead to self-reliance, and one who is self-reliant can always be depended on to do his duty, even under difficult circumstances.

Self-control as to the mind also means concentration on each piece of work as it has to be done. My Master says about the mind: "You must not let it wander. Whatever you are doing, fix your thought upon it, that it may be perfectly done." Much time is lost in school because the boys do not pay sufficient attention to their work; and unless the teacher is himself paying full attention to it the minds of the boys are sure to wander. Prayer and meditation are intended to teach control of the mind, but these are practised only once or twice a day. Unless the mind is controlled all day long by paying attention to everything we do, as the Master directs, we shall never gain real power over our minds, so that they may be perfect instruments.

One of the most difficult parts of a teacher's duty is to turn quickly from one subject to another, as the boys come to him with their different questions and troubles. His mind must be so fully under his control that he can pay complete attention to the particular anxiety of each boy, taking up one after the other with the same care and interest, and without any impatience. If he does not pay this full attention he is sure to make mistakes in the advice which he gives, or to be unjust in his decisions, and out of such mistakes very serious troubles may arise.

On this point my friend, Mr. G. S. Arundale, the well-known Principal of the Central Hindu College, writes: "At frequent intervals, of course, boys come with complaints, with petitions, and here I have to be very careful to concentrate my attention on each boy and on his particular need, for the request, or complaint, or trouble, is sometimes quite trivial and foolish, and yet it may be a great source of worry to the boy unless it is attended to; and even if the boy cannot be satisfied he can generally be sent away contented. One of the most difficult tasks for a teacher is to have sufficient control over his attention to be able continually to turn it from one subject to another without losing intensity, and to bear cheerfully the strain this effort involves. We often speak of something taxing a person's patience, but we really mean that it taxes a person's attention, for impatience is only the desire of the mind to attend to something more interesting than that which for the moment occupies it."

Boys must be helped to concentrate their attention on what they are doing, for their minds are always wandering away from the subject in hand. The world outside them is so full of attractive objects new and interesting to them, that their attention runs away after each fresh thing that comes under their eyes. A child is constantly told to observe, and he takes pleasure in doing so; when he begins to reason he must for the time stop observing and concentrate his mind on the subject he is studying. This change is at first very difficult for him, and the teacher must help him to take up the new attitude. Sometimes attention wanders because the boy is tired, and then the teacher should try to put the subject in a new way. The boy does not generally cease to pay attention wilfully and deliberately, and the teacher must be patient with the restlessness so natural to youth. Let him at least always be sure that the want of attention is not the result of his own fault, of his own way of teaching.

If the attention of the teachers and the boys is trained in this way, the whole school life will become fuller and brighter, and there will be no room for the many harmful thoughts which crowd into the uncontrolled mind. Even when rest is wanted by the mind, it need not be quite empty; in the words of the Master: "Keep good thoughts always in the background of it, ready to come forward the moment it is free."

The Master goes on to explain how the mind may be used to help others, when it has been brought under control. "Think each day of some one whom you know to be in sorrow, or suffering, or in need of help, and pour out loving thoughts upon him." Teachers hardly understand the immense force they may use along this line. They can influence their boys by their thoughts even more than by their words and actions, and by sending out a stream of kind and loving thoughts over the class, the minds of all the boys will be made quieter and happier. Even without speaking a word they will improve the whole atmosphere.

This good influence of thought should spread out from the school over the neighbourhood. As those who live among young people keep young themselves, and keep the ideals and pure aspirations of youth longer than those who live mainly among older people, so the presence of a school should be a source of joy and inspiration to the surrounding neighbourhood or district. Happy and harmonious thought-forms should radiate from it, lighting up the duller atmosphere outside, pouring streams of hope and strength into all within its sphere of influence. The poor should be happier, the sick more comfortable, the aged more respected, because of the school in their midst.

If the teacher often speaks on these subjects to his boys, and from time to time places some clear thought before them, which they all think about together, much good may be done. For thought is a very real and powerful force, especially when many join together with some common thought in their minds. If any great disaster has happened, causing misery to numbers of people, the teacher might take advantage of the religious service to draw attention to the need, and ask the boys to join with him in sending thoughts of love and courage to the sufferers.

The last point mentioned by the Master is pride: "Hold back your mind from pride," He says, "for pride comes only from ignorance." We must not confuse pride with the happiness felt when a piece of work is well done; pride grows out of the feeling of separateness: "*I* have done better than others." Happiness in good work should grow out of the feeling of unity: "I am glad to have done this to help us all." Pride separates a person from others, and makes him think himself superior to those around him; but the pleasure in some piece of work well done is helpful and stimulating, and encourages the doer to take up some more difficult work. When we share with others any knowledge we have gained, we lose all feeling of pride, and the wish to help more, instead of the wish to excel others, becomes the motive for study.

2. *Self-control in action.* The Master points out that while "there must be no laziness, but constant activity in good work ... it must be your *own* duty that you do—not another man's, unless with his permission and by way of helping him." The teacher has, however, a special duty in this connection; for while he must offer to his boys every opportunity for development along their own lines, and must be careful not to check their growth or to force it in an unsuitable direction, he is bound to guide them very carefully, to watch them very closely, and, as Master has said, to tell them gently of their faults. The teacher is in charge of his boys while they are in school, and must, while they are there, take the place of their parents.

His special lesson of self-control is to learn to adapt his own methods to the stage through which his boys are passing. While contenting himself with watching and encouraging them when their activity is running along right lines, he must be ready to step in—with as little disturbance as possible—to modify the activity if it becomes excessive, to stimulate it if it becomes dull, and to turn it into new channels if it has taken a wrong course. In any necessary interposition he should try to make the boys feel that he is helping them to find the way they have missed but really wished to go, rather than forcing them to go his way. Many boys have failed to develop the necessary strength of character, because the teacher, by constant interference, has imposed on them his own knowledge as to right action, instead of trying to awaken their judgment and intuition. The boys become accustomed to depend entirely on him, instead of learning gradually to walk alone.

The teacher must be very careful not to allow outside interests to take him away from his duties in the school. Many teachers do not seem to realise that the school should occupy as much time as they can possibly give to it outside their home duties. They sometimes do the bare amount of work necessary, and then rush away to some other occupation which they find more interesting. No teacher can be really successful in his profession unless it is the thing he cares for most, unless he is eager to devote all the time he can to his boys, and feels that he is happiest when he is working with them or for them.

We are always told that enthusiasm and devotion to their work mark the successful business man, the successful official, the successful statesman; they are equally necessary for the successful teacher. Anyone who desires to rise high in the profession of teaching must bring to his work, not only ability, but similar enthusiasm and devotion. Surely even more enthusiasm and devotion should be brought to the moulding of many hundreds of young lives than to the gaining of money or power. Every moment that the teacher is with his boys he can help them, for, as has always been taught in India, being near a good man helps one's evolution. Away from the school he should be thinking of them and planning for them, and this he cannot do if his whole mind, out of school, is taken up with other interests. On this, again, I may quote Mr. Arundale: "When I get up in the morning my first thought is what has to be done during the day generally and as regards my own work in particular. A rapid mental survey of the School and College enables me to see whether any student seems to stand out as needing particular help. I make a note of any such student in my note book, so that I may call him during the day. Then before College hours, before I take up any extraneous work, I look through my own lectures to see that I am ready far them. By this time students are continually dropping in with questions, with their hopes and aspirations, with difficulties and with troubles, some with slight ailments they want cured. I have a special little place in which to see those young men, so that the atmosphere may be pure and harmonious, and upon each one I endeavour to concentrate my whole attention, shutting everything else completely off, and I am not satisfied unless each boy leaves me with a smile upon his face."

Unless a teacher works in this spirit, he does not understand how sacred and solemn a trust is placed in his hands. No teacher is worthy of the name who does not realise that he serves God most truly and his country most faithfully when he lives and works with his boys. His self-sacrificing life, lived amongst them, inspires them to perform their duties well, as they see him performing his, and thus they grow in reverence and patriotism. These boys are God's children entrusted to his care; they are the hope of the nation placed in his hands. How shall he answer to God and the nation, when the trust passes out of his hands, if he has not consecrated his whole time and thought to discharge it faithfully, but has allowed the boys to go out into the world with out love to God, and without the wish and power to serve their country?

Boys, as well as teachers, must learn self-control in action. They must not so engage in other activities as to neglect their ordinary school duties. My Master says to those who wish to serve Him: "You must do ordinary work better than others, not worse." A boy's first duty in school is to learn well, and nothing should lead him to neglect his regular school work. Outside this—as it is best that his activities should be kept within the school—the wise teacher will provide within the school organisation all the activities in which his boys can usefully take part. If there should be any national organisation to which he thinks it useful that they should belong, he will himself organise a branch of it within the school and he himself and the other teachers will take part in it. For example the Boy-Scout movement and the Sons of India are both national organisations, but branches of them should be formed in the separate schools. Teachers should train their boys to realise that just as the home is the centre of activity for the child, so is the school the centre of activity for the youth. As the child draws his life and energy from the home, so the youth should draw his from the school. The most useful work should be done in connection with the school so that it may form part of the general education of the boy, and be in harmony with the rest of his growth. There should be in the school debating societies, in which the rules of debate are carefully observed, so that the boys may learn self-control in argument; dramatic clubs in which they may learn control of expression; athletic clubs in which control of mind and action are both acquired; literary societies for boys specially interested in certain studies; societies for helping the poorer students.

It is also very important to give the boys an opportunity of understanding the conditions under which their country is growing, so that in the school they may practice patriotism apart from politics. It is very unfortunate that in India students are often taught by unscrupulous agitators that love of their country should be shown by hatred of other countries; the boys would never believe this, if their own school provided patriotic services for its boys, so as to give a proper outlet for the enthusiasm they rightly feel. They only seek an outlet away from the school because none is provided for them within it.

Groups of students should be formed for various kinds of social service according to the capacities of the boys, and the needs of their surroundings: for the protection of animals, for rendering first aid to the injured, for the education of the depressed classes, for service in connection with national and religious festivals, and so on. Boys, for whom such forms of service are provided in their schools, will not want to carry them on separately.

Boys have a special opportunity of practising self-control in action when they play games. The boys come from the more formal discipline of the class-room into conditions in which there is a sudden cessation of external authority; unless they have learned to replace this with self-control, we shall see in the play-ground brutality in the stronger followed by fear in the weaker. The playing fields have a special value in arousing the power of self-discipline, and if teachers are there who set the example of submitting to the authority of the captain, of showing gentleness and honour, and playing for the side rather than for themselves, they will much help the boys in gaining self-control.

The boys also will see the teacher in a new light; he is no longer imposing his authority upon them as a teacher, but he is ruling himself from within and subordinating his own action to the rules of the game, and to the interests of those who are playing with him. The boy who enters the field with no other idea than that of enjoying himself as much as he can, even at the expense of his fellow-students, will learn from his teacher's example that he is happiest when playing for others, not for himself alone, and that he plays best when the object of the game is the honour of the school and not his own advantage. He also learns that the best player is the boy who practises his strokes carefully, and uses science to direct strength. Desiring to be a good player himself, he begins to train his body to do as he wishes, thus gaining self-control in action; through this self-control he learns the great lesson, that self-control increases happiness and leads to success.

Another thing learned in the play-ground is control of temper, for a boy who loses his temper always plays badly. He learns not to be hasty and impatient, and to control his speech even when he is losing, and not to show vanity when he wins. Thus he is making a character, strong and well-balanced, which will be very useful to him when he comes to be a man. All this is really learned better in the play-ground than in the class-room.

3. *Tolerance*. Most of my Master's directions under this head are intended mainly for disciples, but still their spirit may be applied to those who are living the ordinary life. Tolerance is a virtue which is very necessary in schools, especially when the scholars are of different faiths. "You must feel," says my Master, "perfect tolerance for all, and a hearty interest in the beliefs of those of another religion, just as much as in your own. For their

religion is a path to the highest just as yours is. And to help all you must understand all." It is the duty of the teacher to be the first in setting an example along these lines.

Many teachers, however, make the mistake of thinking that the views and rules to which they are themselves accustomed are universal principles which everybody ought to accept. They are therefore anxious to destroy the students' own convictions and customs, in order to replace them by others which they think better. This is especially the case in countries like India, where the boys are of many religions. Unless the teacher studies sympathetically the religions of his pupils, and understands that the faith of another is as dear to him as his own is to himself, he is likely to make his boys unbelievers in all religion. He should take special care to speak with reverence of the religions to which his boys belong, strengthening each in the great principles of his own creed, and showing the unity of all religions by apt illustrations taken from the various sacred books. Much can be done in this direction during the religious service which precedes the ordinary work of the day, if this be carried out on lines common to all; while each boy should be taught the doctrines of his own religion, it would be well if he were reminded once in the day of the unity of all religions, for, as the Master said, every "religion is a path to the highest."

An example would thus be set in the school of members of different religions living happily side by side, and showing respect to each other's opinions. I feel that this is one of the special functions of the school in the life of the nation. At home the boy is always with those who hold the same opinions as himself, and he has no opportunity of coming into touch with other beliefs and other customs. At school he should have the opportunity of meeting other ways of believing, and the teacher should lead him to understand these, and to see the unity underneath them. The teacher must never make a boy discontented with his own faith by speaking contemptuously of it, or by distorting it through his own ignorance. Such conduct on his part leads a boy to despise all religion.

Then again there are many different customs which belong to the different parts of the country. People often exaggerate these and look on them as essential parts of religion instead of only as marks of the part of the country in which they were born. Hence they look with contempt or disapproval on those whose customs differ from their own, and they keep themselves proudly separate. I do not know how far this is a difficulty in western countries, but in India I think that customs separate us much more than physical distance or religious differences. Each part of the country has its own peculiarities as to dress, as to the manner of taking food, as to the way of wearing the hair, school boys are apt at first to look down upon those of their schoolfellows whose appearance or habits differ from their own. Teachers should help boys to get over these trivial differences and to think instead of the one Motherland to which they all belong.

We have already said that patriotism should be taught without race hatred, and we may add that understanding and loving other nations is part of the great virtue of tolerance. Boys are obliged to learn the history of their own and of other nations; and history, as it is taught, is full of wars and conquests. The teacher should point out how much terrible suffering has been caused by these, and that though, in spite of them, evolution has made its way and has even utilised them, far more can be gained by peace and good will than by hatred. If care is taken to train children to look on different ways of living with interest and sympathy instead of with distrust and dislike, they will grow up into men who will show to all nations respect and tolerance.

4. *Cheerfulness*. No teacher who really loves his students can be anything but cheerful during school hours. No brave man will allow himself to be depressed, but depression is particularly harmful in a teacher, for he is daily in contact with many boys, and he spreads among them the condition of his own mind. If the teacher is depressed the boys cannot long be cheerful and happy; and unless they are cheerful and happy they cannot learn well. If teachers and boys associate cheerfulness with their school life, they will not only find the work easier than it would otherwise be, but they will turn to the school as to a place in which they can for the time live free from all cares and troubles.

The teacher should train himself to turn away from all worrying and depressing thoughts the moment he enters the school gate, for his contribution to the school atmosphere, in which the boys must live and grow, must be cheerfulness and energy. The best way to get rid of depression is to occupy the mind with something bright and interesting, and this should not be difficult when he is going to his boys. Thoughts die when no attention is paid to them so it is better to turn away from depressing thoughts than to fight them. Cheerfulness literally increases life, while depression diminishes it, and by getting rid of depression the teacher increases his energy. It is often indeed very difficult for the teacher, who has the cares of family life upon him, to keep free from anxiety, but still he must try not to bring it into the school.

Mr. Arundale tells me that he has made a habit of becoming cheerful the moment he enters the College gates, however worried he may have been beforehand, because, he writes: "I want my contribution to the school day to be happiness and interest, and by a daily process of making myself pretend to be cheerful when the College gates are entered, I have finally succeeded in becoming so. If, as I pass through the grounds to my office, I see any student looking dull and gloomy, I make a point of going up to him in order to exert my cheerfulness against his gloom, and the gloom soon passes away. Then comes the religious service, and when I take my seat upon the platform with the religious instructor, I try to ask the Master's blessing on all the dear young faces I see before me, and I look slowly around upon each member of the audience, trying to send out a continual stream of affection and sympathy."

I have already said that boys watch their teachers' faces to see if they are in a good or a bad mood. If the teacher is always cheerful and loving, the boys will no longer watch him, for they will have learned to trust him, and all anxiety and strain will disappear. If the teacher displays constant cheerfulness, he sends out among his boys streams of energy and good will, new life pours into them, their attention is stimulated, and the sympathy of the teacher conquers the carelessness of the boy.

Just as a boy learns control of action on the play-ground, so he may learn there this virtue of cheerfulness. To be cheerful in defeat makes the character strong, and the boy who can be cheerful and good-tempered in the face of the team which has just defeated him is well on the way to true manliness.

5. *One-pointedness.* One-pointedness, the concentration of attention on each piece of work as it is being done, so that it may be done as well as possible, largely depends upon interest. Unless the teacher is interested in his work, and loves it beyond all other work, he will not be able to be really one-pointed. He must be so absorbed in his school duties that his mind is continually occupied in planning for his boys, and looks upon everything in the light of its possible application to his own particular work.

One-pointedness means enthusiasm, but enthusiasm is impossible without ideals. So the teacher who desires to be one-pointed must be full of ideals to which he is eager to lead his school. These ideals will sharpen his attention, and make him able to concentrate it even upon quite trivial details. He will have the ideal school in his mind, and will always be trying to bring the real school nearer to it. To be one-pointed, therefore, the teacher must not be contented with things as they are, but must be continually on the alert to take advantage of every opportunity of improvement.

The teacher's ideal will of course be modified as he learns more of his students' capacities and of the needs of the nation. In this way, as the years pass, the teacher may find himself far from the early ideals that at first gave him one-pointedness. Ideals will still guide him, but they will be more practical, and so his one-pointedness will be much keener and will produce larger results.

The Master quotes two sayings which seem to me to show very clearly the lines along which one-pointedness should work: "Whatsoever thy hand findeth to do, do it with thy might"; and: "Whatsoever ye do, do it *heartily*, as to the Lord and not unto men." It must be done "as to the Lord." The Master says: "Every piece of work must be done religiously—done with the feeling that it is a sacred offering to be laid on the altar of the Lord. 'This do I, O Lord, in Thy name and for Thee.' Thinking this, can I offer to Him anything but my very best? Can I let *any* piece of my work be done carelessly or inattentively, when I know that it is being done expressly for Him? Think how you would do your work if you knew that the Lord Himself were coming directly to see it; and then realise that He *does* see it, for all is taking place within His consciousness. So will you do your duty 'as unto the Lord and not as unto men'."

The work must be done, too, according to the teacher's knowledge of the principles of evolution, and not merely out of regard to small and fleeting interests. The teacher must therefore gradually learn his own place in evolution, so that he may become one-pointed as to himself; unless he practises one-pointedness with regard to his own ideal for himself, he will not be able to bring it to bear on his surroundings. He must try to be in miniature the ideal towards which he hopes to lead his boys, and the application of the ideal to himself will enable him to see in it details which otherwise would escape his notice, or which he might neglect as unimportant.

The practical application, then, of one-pointedness lies in the endeavour to keep before the mind some dominant central ideal towards which the whole of the teachers' and boys' daily routine shall be directed, so that the small life may be vitalised by the larger, and all may become conscious parts of one great whole. The ideal of service, for instance, may be made so vivid that the whole of daily life shall be lived in the effort to serve.

6. *Confidence*. First among the qualifications for the teacher has been placed Love, and it is fitting that this little book should end with another qualification of almost equal importance—Confidence. Unless the teacher has confidence in his power to attain his goal, he will not be able to inspire a similar confidence in his boys, and self-confidence is an indispensable attribute for success in all departments of human activity. The Master has beautifully explained why we have the right to be confident.

"You must trust yourself. You say you know yourself too well? If you feel so, you do *not* know yourself; you know only the weak outer husk, which has fallen often into the mire. But *you*—the real you—you are a spark of God's own fire, and God, Who is almighty, is in you, and because of that there is nothing that you cannot do if you will."

The teacher must feel that he has the power to teach his boys and to train them for their future work in the world. This power is born of his love for them and his desire to help them, and is drawn from the one spiritual life of which all partake. It is because the teacher and his boys are one in essence, make one little flame in "God's own fire," that the teacher has the right to be confident that every effort to help, growing out of his own share in the one life, will reach and stimulate that same life in the boys.

He will not always be able to see at once the effect he is producing. Indeed, the most important influence the teacher has shows itself in the growing characters of the boys. No success in examinations, in reports, in inspections can satisfy the real teacher as to the effect of his work. But when he feels that his own higher nature is strengthened and purified by his eagerness to serve his boys, when he has the joy of watching the divine life in them shining out in answer to that in himself, then his happiness is indeed great. Then he has the peace of knowing that he has awakened in his boys the knowledge of their own divinity, which, sooner or later, will bring them to perfection.

The teacher is justified in feeling confident because the divine life is in him and his boys, and they turn to him for inspiration and strength. Let him but send out to them all that is highest in himself, and he may be quite sure that there will not be one boy who will not to some extent respond in his own higher Self, however little the response may be seen by the teacher.

This constant interplay of the one life between teacher and students will draw them ever nearer to each other. They learn in the school to live together as elder and younger brothers of the one school family. By living a life of brotherhood within the small area of the school, they will be trained to live that life in the larger area of the nation. Then they will gradually learn that there is but one great brotherhood in all the world, one divine life in all. This life each separate member of the brotherhood is trying to express, consciously or unconsciously. The teacher is indeed happy who knows his own divinity; that knowledge of the divinity in man is the highest lesson it will ever be his privilege to teach.